Copyright © 2019 Tekkan
Artwork Copyright © 2019

All rights reserved.
First Printing, 2019
ISBN 978-1-7324107-9-4

To contact Tekkan please email:
buddhaboy1289@gmail.com

Table of Contents

Google and Facebook . . . . Page 80

Aslan . . . . Page 88

Appearances . . . . Page 99

How to Read My Poems

I have married the sonnet to the tanka. I tell a story in the sonnet — using three quatrains, separated by line spaces, and a final couplet. The story builds to a conclusion in the couplet. The tanka is a commentary, or a counterpoint, to the sonnet — the combined poems have two endings.

I don't rhyme my sonnets, because I want freer expression. I want to be direct in my meaning — I want people to clearly understand my meaning. The metaphors are inspired by Shakespeare, and the (aimed-for) precision is in imitation of Japanese style. Using the sonnet with the tanka, I am mixing the sensibility of the Occident and the Orient — which I have done by living in England, Japan, and America.

I don't punctuate much in my poetry. I want the words themselves to do the work. There is logic between words, and the forms provide structure. By not using punctuation I hope to direct readers to carefully attend to each word — to appreciate the graininess of words.

Reading my poems silently, say, on a bus, a train, or an airplane, and reading them aloud, may be different experiences. The way I've written there's not always a pause intended at the end of the line. Hint: *My poems are to be recited not as lines, but as phrases, and a phrase often overflows the break at the end of a line. I pause and take a breath where it seems natural for me to pause. Another person may pause differently than I do.*

Each single poem is a piece of a mosaic, and it is my hope that the collection of poems form an accurate portrait of consciousness.

My daughter, Jocelyn MacDonald, is a wonderful artist. Her art work graces this book.

I am Barry MacDonald. I received the *dharma* name, *Tekkan*, which means, Iron Man, a settled practitioner of great determination.

— *Tekkan*

Everyday Mind IX

The harvest moon
was large and orange
on the horizon —
it is small and silver
this morning.

I knew that people needed bifocals
When they get older but I believed that
My eyes wouldn't be effected — but then
I became irritated with the small

Printing of the books I was reading and
My eyes began to hurt from looking at
A computer screen at work — and now I
Occasionally close my eyes and rest while

Listening to my surroundings knowing
What aging feels like and accepting that
Sometimes the world will appear blurred and
Watery to me until my eyesight

Sharpens again as I am learning how
To pace the use of my abilities.

Birds clouds
autumn leaves
the warm expressions
of my friends are
more precious.

I've gotten used to being present and
Listening while a group is having a
Lively conversation because it does
Happen that they have more in common with

Each other then I do with them — and I've
Put up with the discomfort that comes with
Feeling separate from people — but I
Am refining my morning clarity

When I settle with my desk and keyboard
Along with my containers of coffee
And I play with perceptions by finding
The words that fit well together and in

The play there is a hunt for worthiness —
There is something worth articulating.

Within the
ordinary
there is the
extraordinary.

I knew it was the last time that I would
Meet with Zen Master Harada at a
Temple in the town of Obama on
A bay by the Sea of Japan because

I was returning to America —
And we were sitting on the tatami
Together in the Japanese style for
Our last words — and my abdomen filled with

A sudden warmth as we faced each other
And the warmth originated from the
Zen Master as he demonstrated the
Love and power of the emptiness from

Which everything arises — and thirty
Years later the warmth resides within me.

There are times when I
forget the inspiration
of that moment but
there is a connection now
that can never be broken.

I was surprised this morning by the frost
That needed to be scraped from my windshield
Because I was in a hurry and was
Not prepared to have the time taken from

Me — and on my way around town I see
The party colors of the autumn leaves
Emerging and already the season
Is cooler while spring seemed to have arrived

Yesterday — and at home I will raise the
Screen windows and lower the outward glass
So that the double panes of glass of each
Window are in place for the winter cold —

I won't need the dehumidifier
But will have to rely on the furnace.

An air of
seriousness
and severity
is settling
over Stillwater.

There is always a horizon in the
Distance and the permutations of the
Sky are continuous — and I am not
Separate from this overcast morning

But the gloom is counterbalanced with the
Yellow and orange and scarlet leaves — and
I remember tulips by the garage
The apple blossoms by the driveway and

The lilacs on the corner and it seems
Like yesterday I was measuring the
Amount of shoveling necessary with
My first step out of the door and into

The snow and the snow was heavy and deep
And I knew that I would be struggling.

The break from the rain
the dampness in the air and
the gray of the sky
from which the water will drop
are a weight upon my mind.

It is ironic that in English the
Word "hole" beginning with the letter
"H" represents a nothingness and yet
The word "Whole" beginning with the letter

"W" — a doubling of a "u" —
Indicates something that is complete and
Harmonious within itself — so that
The same sound spelled differently indicates

Both absence and an inclusive presence —
And it is evocative that in the
Middle of the Milky Way there is a
Black hole with enough gravity to spin

A hundred billion stars about itself
At one point three million miles per hour.

The Buddhists say
in emptiness there is form
and in form there is
emptiness.

The grass is soaked with overnight rain and
The sky has been overcast this morning
But the clouds are separating and the
Sun is appearing and disappearing

As we are in the twilight time of the
Seasons again on the verge of longer
Nights and for me the quality of light
Becomes precious — as just for a moment

I saw the edges of a bank of clouds
Lit by the sun before a mass of gray
Obscured my view — and it is true even
In winter I cannot look directly

At the sun without damaging my eyes
But I will enjoy the reflected sun.

The leaves are in
autumn colors
and aren't falling
yet but it is
inevitable.

I am doing what is possible to
Expand my circle of acquaintance and
Now that I've composed several books and want
To market them I am meeting poets

At poetry readings where we share each
Others' vision and enthusiasm —
And this group meets once a month and perhaps
I'm off balance and assuming too much

But I sense guardedness amongst us as
If we were competing for attention
And status of ability were up
For grabs — and I want admiration —

But I'm also lonely and looking for
Companions and lively exploration.

Every single day
there is something worth
remembering and
communication
aids intuition.

Today I am enjoying my little
Bubble of consciousness on a rainy
Day in October by imagining
Piles of snow along the streets as I am

Driving to meet my circle of sober
Alcoholics — because I know there will
Be an hour of honest and healthy
Discussion — and no matter what gloomy

Encumbrance I arrive with I know
From experience my troubles will melt
Away once I sit among companions
And practice listening and when it is

My turn to speak with the intention of
Being positive I am positive.

Enthusiasm
is easier with
companions and
with ears.

The key to my Japanese car does have
A blade that would fit in the keyway of
The door but I have never used my key
That way — instead I push a button and

Waves emanate from the key and unlock
The door automatically — and in the
Morning and evening I am sending
Text messages and photos to a friend in

Sri Lanka by touching the screen of my
Phone with my fingers and through the air my
Thoughts and emotions and the images
I like arrive instantaneously

Around the earth — and I am waking up
In bed and she is in the evening.

Emotions are
sticky and
digestion and
comprehension
are tricky.

It is already cold enough to chill
In the early days of October and
The wind has a biting edge and the swift
Gray clouds are coalescing into an

Overcast sky of impending storm but
Most of the leaves haven't fallen and I
Haven't cut and bagged the daylilies and
Hostas and haven't mowed the grass for a

Final time — I am accustomed to the
Timely passage of leaves and I enjoy
The regularity of my outside
Chores as if by emptying gas from the

Lawn mower and by changing the oil in
The snow blower I am really ready.

The leaves are
brilliantly colored —
and soon the wind
will be howling through
the bare branches.

My mind is a bowl I am holding in
My hands attending to the arising
Of my thinking — and the politics of
Today is poisonous with villains and

Saviors and battles without end — and I
Am digesting detailed controversy
Desiring the triumph of goodness
Witnessing emotional distortions

And flammable opinions without the
Possibility of moderation —
And I am organizing my point of
View and marshalling an array of facts

To satisfy an urge for clarity
But I am also wanting a release.

While cutting and bagging
daylilies and hostas
in preparation for
winter I will gently
dissipate bitterness.

I will pluck all of the apples from the
Tree that I can reach and let the others
Fall to feed the squirrels — and I will seize
The Hostas and daylilies and cut and

Bag them — my legs will give me leverage
My back and arms will be pulling — my right
Hand will grasp — and my left will slice with
A bright steel blade — and tomorrow my legs

And back will punish me and I will have
Difficulty moving for several
Days — and after the exuberance of
Activity has worn off my fingers

Will ache and the swollen areas will
Inform me where splitters are embedded.

When I am cutting
and bagging I will seize this
sunny afternoon
to indulge vibrant and
exhilarated thinking.

The African elephants have floppy
Ears while Asian elephants have tiny
Ears but both the African and Asian
Elephants can detect the lumbering

Presence of far away elephants by
"Listening" to the plodding of thudding
Elephant feet emanating in the
Waves from every elephant foot that stomps

On the earth — but the elephant doesn't
Hear elephants thumping with its ears but
It measures the distance of its plopping
Cousins through the bottom of its feet as

It stands in place tickled by vibrations
Stimulating its marvelous flatness.

The wrinkles around
an elephant's eyes suggest
wisdom but with its
wrapping and grasping trunk it
behaves mischievously.

The destroying edge of the eye wall of
A hurricane wrenches a broad swath of
Habitation — but the narrow focus
Of a tornado is personal when

A family's home is ripped apart but a
Neighbor's is not — and the downpour of a
Hurricane saturates the valleys and
Floods the streets and homes with enveloping

Devastation — bringing sudden change — but
Such lightning fractures are not the subjects
Of my poetry because they haven't
Happened to me and so how could I be

Authentic in description — so I will
Write about the cumulative changes.

There is an
accumulation of
snow this morning
with the leaves resolutely
clinging to the trees.

Because the cats are so insistent I
Feed them right after waking up in the
Morning but today I changed the routine
And brushed them beforehand and they made the

Same noise as always — and I am used to
Doing my chores in regular order —
But I am discovering the order
Is arbitrary and I am doing

What I want in another sequence in
The same amount time — if I shave and
Shower before breakfast I won't be late —
And once I am soaping under a stream

Of clarifying water my thinking
Will reveal what is important today.

Often I am
exuberant but
sometimes there is
an urgency
to succeed.

I've been trying to explain with thousands
Of words the experience of seeking
For inspiration in ordinary
Events so very easy to discount

And I believe it was necessary
For me to cross a threshold of pain and
Dissatisfaction — and I was lucky
To realize my spirit was growing

Under the pressure of adversity —
And I was surprised that my bitterness
Was dissolving when I joined a circle
Of friends and I began listening to

How they turned their difficulties over
To wisdom surpassing comprehension.

So much trouble
comes from wanting
what I really
don't need.

With the passage of the several months
Since the removal of the cottonwood
Outside the window where I assemble
My thoughts into words on paper I can

See so much more sunrise pouring over
The neighboring trees — the light is slanting
Across my view and lighting the leaves from
An angle and leaving most of the trees

In shadow — the light is mixing with the
Autumn colors and where it is touching
The leaves passing through a blue sky there is
Joyous brilliance that lightens my heart and

Miles away I can enjoy the tiny
White contrails of a jetliner drifting.

Within two weeks the
leaves will be down and through
bare branches the far
edge of the river valley
will become visible.

This room where I work is disorganized
With things that are no longer useful to
The operation of the business like
The envelope collating machine and

The light table for laying out copy
To be printed — and there are cobwebs in
The corners of the windows and dust is
Collecting on the books in the shelves — but

The light coming into the windows and
Illuminating the hundreds of things
And the light revealing the ten thousand
Things within sight outside of the windows

Every day is the light enlivening
Everything that ever lived on the earth.

In daylight there is
an overlay of
stimulation and
vibrancy easy
to overlook.

Today we are experiencing the
Twilight season of the year preparing
For the months when the wind is howling in
The bare branches and snow has overcome

The ground but that is not what's happening
Now as I am walking by the river
Over the Crossing Bridge and back to my
Home in Stillwater — I am watching the

Afternoon sun sparkle among the red
And yellow and orange leaves in a breeze
And the leaves are falling in the breeze and
This will be my last long walk when it is

Possible this year to see a golden
Burst of the sun flicker among the leaves.

Everyday
more light and
vitality
is draining
from daylight.

I was watching a video on my
Phone of a juvenile elephant in
A creek with muddy and slippery banks —
The youngster wanted out and came to a

Sloping spot and not too steep — and thrusting
Upwards and flopping sideways onto the
Bank the elephant reached a tipping point
Several times but just couldn't get over —

Looking like a chubby kid struggling
Up the wall on an obstacle course and
Failing — in befuddlement and distress
The adolescent wavered in the creek

Until an adult ambling over
And stepping into the creek helped him out.

The elephant
used his massive
head to push
from behind and
they escaped.

The branches are brown under a gray sky
And drops of rain are falling here and there
Into the grass that is sodden and green —
And red and yellow leaves are on the street

And I am seeing the birds frolicking
In the air as a group turning in an
Instant and stopping in a bare tree — and
Then they fly again turning together

As if they were of one mind and then they
Vanish — and the last leaves are descending
Singly and severally in the wind
And I can see a rainy haze on the

Horizon across the river valley —
And it is not cold enough to snow yet.

The birds frolic
as if the gray sky
were not concerning
and air and branches
were eternal.

It's perplexing that in the transition
Into winter there is a blooming of
Vibrancy when the white and grey of a
Cloud rapidly blowing in the blue of

The sky makes a stunning contrast — when just
Moments ago the finest flakes of snow
Were descending — and I question why when
The leaves of each tree are revealing the

Most brilliant yellows oranges and reds
Something irrepressible inside me
Awakens with joyful celebration
As if today were a festival of

Natural beauty — while my bare hands are
Chilled to the bone by a persisting wind.

It happens that the
severity of winter
is proceeded by
a reverberation of
exuberant piquancy.

When a problem without an emerging
Solution is in my way I don't have
To worry because soon I will cross my
Legs and meditate — and I don't sit with

The intention of solving my problems
And there is the freedom to think about
Whatever I want — but I have come to
Enjoy watching my thoughts in transition

And energy envelopes my thinking
And transforms my inclinations over
Time so when a persisting conundrum
Or an emotional snare arises

I am good at regaining my balance
Because I have dissolving energy.

Releasing
energy
underlies
experience
transforming
experience.

There is a cottonwood on the corner
Of my yard that drops its leaves later than
The other surrounding trees on the cusp
Of November — and a quarter of the

Leaves have fallen but it will take a week
For all of them to go — and this morning
The slanting light caught the yellow leaves and
Produced a glowing orange and there was

Not any wind — I was leaving home on
The way to work thinking about how to
Apportion the chores that need doing with
My limited time including raking

The cottonwood leaves and bagging leaves for
The waste disposal pickup on Thursday.

The yellowest leaves
on a frosty morning were
suffused in slanting
transitory sunlight but
now the sight is vanishing.

Apart from the persona I assume
When composing my poems I do have
A nervous disposition as I rush
From one chore to another — and there are

Emails to read and write and essays to
Consider once I'm done with laundry
And cooking eating and washing dishes —
And the once in a while intrusions — like

Calling the accountant and maintaining
The car and raking leaves — are as constant
As clouds drifting along in the sky — but
When I'm attending to the clouds I am

Serene though when doing chores I can be
Resentfully harassed and distracted.

I can also be
the juggler with
busy hands tossing
my chores
happily.

Yesterday I communicated with
You about being just too jittery and
Distracted and I could not have written
Otherwise because I was in the midst

Of unavoidable bustle with not
Enough time in the day — and the haste of
The moment had to be balanced by the
Need to choose my words carefully — and the

Words came with difficulty but they fell
Into place eventually so that
Even though I hurried through the rest of
The day I could cherish a smidgen of

Satisfaction because in difficult
Circumstances I did find expression.

I can't wrench
myself into peaceful
thinking — but I
can learn to surf
turbulent emotions.

It wouldn't be correct to believe that
I am a master of myself because
That would suggest that serenity comes
Easily to me — but at least when I

Am nervous I recognize nervousness —
When conflicted with many thoughts going
In too many directions I do know
At the moment it would be better if

I could slow down a little — and I am
Surprised by the strength of my emotions
But I don't try to ignore or suppress
Them anymore and if I am careful

Even in the midst of activity
I can resonate with satisfaction.

I respond to
circumstances
and am better
at regaining
composure.

There was rain and wind in the night and in
The morning most of the leaves were on the
Ground and seeing the newly bare branches
Again is a stark indication of

The bleak season before us but I will
Use several afternoons to rake and bag
The leaves as active meditation to
Reflect during the exercise of my

Body on what I am doing now that
Increases my dissatisfaction — I
Usually know if I am honest
With myself when I am doing something

That can only lead to unhappiness
And what would be a better direction.

Pulling the rake
clearing the ground
collecting the leaves
bending and bagging
gathering willingness.

When the bare branches are revealed in
In the pale blue sky of a cold morning
And the light is brilliant in the leaves of
A few trees that are holding on for the

Last hour I savor a melancholy
Pleasure in the draining away of the
Vibrancy of summer — and the birds that
Were singing with the rising sun are gone —

And the grass isn't growing — and the leaves
That were yellow a few days ago on
My cottonwood were brown on the ground — and
Now they are in bags along the street to

Be disposed of — today I have only
One blister on my hand from raking leaves.

But a blue sky is
always full of light
and even on a
cold overcast day
I generate warmth.

I know the sun is ninety-three million
Miles away and gravity is crushing
Inward on the core and resulting in
Nuclear fusion and combustion and

A photon of light and energy is
Colliding with other photons for ten
Million years before it emerges from
The core to the surface of the sun — and

It only takes eight minutes to reach the
Earth — and I know every living being
On the earth lives by the grace of the sun
And the sun has always been a giver

Of warmth and life and consciousness even
On a cloudy day in early winter.

It is the same
radiance on my
cottonwood that
moved people to build
Stonehenge.

The crows are always in the trees or on
The ground in threes or fours by the carcass
Of a rabbit in the grass or stabbing
A dead squirrel on the road — and they will

Fly away as I drive by — and I do
Hear their harsh voices coming in the open
Windows in the summer and imagine
The imposition of dominance in

Crow language — but when the leaves are down and
The branches are starkly bare again their
Black presence in the trees or on the ground
Reveals the return of the barren days

When the sunlight is less prominent and
And an icy wind is in the branches.

There is
austere beauty
in the rising sun
in the bare branches.

Chickadees are messy eaters he said
And he has two tubular feeders in
His yard and the chickadees empty one
A week — and he will be working in the

Yard and they will be flitting back and forth
But when he looks at them they will stop and
Scatter — he lives in a wooded hollow
And in the winter he sees chickadees

Nut hatches yellow-bellied sapsuckers
Sparrows pileated woodpeckers and
Cardinals — and he is ambling through
His days and aware of how lucky he

Is because where I go there are only
The crows stabbing carcasses on the street.

Before the sunrise
a pink light is along the
horizon beyond the
river valley visible
because the leaves have fallen.

It happens at the gym with people I
See now and then after saying hello
To each other for months finally we
Introduce ourselves and I walk away

Grateful to have made another friend and
Then the days or weeks go by without our
Meeting — but then I see him again and
Realize I can't remember his name

So I scurry out of sight before he
Sees me — and I don't want him to suppose
His name is not worthy enough of
My remembering it — and I am so

Ashamed of myself for my forgetting
But there is no getting around the fact.

And it happens at
the gym that sometimes I can
remember someone's
name and they are forgetting
mine — and I am quite relieved.

Eventually my forgetting of
A name needs to be remedied because
I am on friendly terms with everyone
So I make an admission and I hear

The name repeated and I resort to
Tricks — sometimes I may connect a person
With the name of a famous person or
With a friend who has the very same name —

And sometimes I may identify a
Prominent feature such as with Nosey
Nolan or Boisterous Bob — but then it's
Imperative that I remember though

Perhaps my earnest effort doesn't help
And makes remembering more difficult.

I also try to
suppress thoughts
inadvertently
producing
obsession.

There is a bush warbler in Japan I
Heard while walking along a mountain path
In spring — and I never saw the bird but
Its sound was a liquid loveliness that

Was otherworldly — and the Japanese
Call it the *uguisu* and the name
Is an attempt to recreate its song
But that is impossible to do with

Syllables because the warbler doesn't
Repeat a pattern and people aren't birds
And every instance the *uguisu*
Sings the sound is a once-in-a-lifetime

Penetration of the day and thirty
Years later I remember its effect.

I recall the
vaguest memory of
fascination.

The *uguisu* was hidden in my
Memory until I read a volume
Of poetry by Ryokan who was
A Japanese Zen monk who lived in a

Hermitage in the mountains and who wrote
That his poems were not poems — and when
He described sitting by a banana
Tree that seemed to be sweeping clouds away

And cooling his hut with shade he conveyed
The moment with an uncluttered heart and
He wasn't thinking about practicing
Zen but he was immersed in reading the

Wordless verses of nature absorbing
Drifting illusion and enlightenment.

The sound of the
uguisu happens
as everything
is arising
at once.

The aftermath of an election is
A revelation every time when the
Winning coalitions and strategies
Are determined and the operatives

Can never be secure by deploying
Superior knowledge or gamesmanship
Because the voting public is fickle
And emotion and loyalty can shift

And once a person assumes a point of
View in every national election
Virtuous candidates lose and scoundrels
Prevail in some locations — and it is

Necessary that the voters bear the
Consequences and hopefully they learn.

Snow is covering
the bare branches this morning
so I put on a
wool hat and boots and mittens
and a warm winter jacket.

It would be easy in November to
Let the imposition of a gray sky
Overwhelm my outlook without even
Being consciously aware of the shift

In my attitude — going about my
Business I settle into the drab browns
Of the trees without their leaves with the thin
Layer of the first snow on the ground and

With the sudden arrival of the cold
That clings to every movement I make when
Without noticing much I calculate
Whether gloves are necessary while I'm

Handling thermoses of coffee and
Aiming the key to turn and lock my door.

The experience
of a gray November sky
settling upon
my mind imposing the cold
again is worth noticing.

From one day to the next things may appear
Differently and this morning the branches
Have a coating of snow and the sky is
White with just a tinge of gray — and behind

My home there is a birch that throughout the
Summer I seldom notice because its
White bark is overwhelmed by the sun and
The grass and leaves and the blue of the sky

And there is always a dog barking and
The birds are about — but in the stillness
Of morning the white paper birch blends in
With its brown branches and twigs and with the

Snow on the ground it epitomizes
The beauty of a quiet winter day.

Tromping along
after the first snowfall
and making my first
boot prints in the snow I am
pioneering the landscape.

A friend sent a book of Buddhist wisdom
From Sri Lanka and last evening I read
Much familiar *dharma* — and I liked the
Perspective that science may dissect the

Material world but has no leverage
Over the dynamics of the mind and
Consciousness — and I was reminded of
The necessity of understanding the

Law of karma that I must live with the
Consequences of my predilections
But when I woke this morning I recalled
Her point — we can't purify the world we

Can only purify ourselves — and the
Urge to dominate causes suffering.

For twenty-five years
I've been editing a
political journal
chastising peoples'
mischievous behavior.

The gift of inspiration is the best
That we may give each other and I am
Capable of giving after having
My measure of suffering and after

Having some insight into the cause of
The suffering — and I am grateful to
Have my circle of friends and the room where
We meet — and I am lucky we practice

Our listening without interruption
And it does take practice to understand
The turning points that warped the lens I use
For seeing and if I do carefully

Listen then I may recognize enough
Similarity and be insightful.

Honesty without
the imposition of
advice is sufficient
for receiving clarity
and creating gratitude.

There is a book about recovery
From addiction and alcoholism
With many fine expressions and words well
Worth the reading about what it means to

Have a spirit capable of growing
Beyond the grasping and frightened ego
But for me the best thing about the book
Is the photo on the cover of an

Asphalt road turning within a forest
With the sunlight bursting in the trees and
Symbolizing the glowing fact of life
That I may choose to pursue a path that

Is founded on the assumption of a
Goodness that I may grow my roots into.

The choice is mine
whether to allow
parasitic thoughts and
lethargy to consume me
or to follow the way.

There is a trick that goes on in the
Political world that's great for gaining
Leverage and momentum and that is
To assume self-righteousness and then to

Accuse the target of inhumanity
And all the attention of the public
Seizes on the accusation and the
Villainous character of the supposed

Malefactor — and the cunning and motives
Of the accuser are overlooked in the
Defamation of the target — and the
Combustion of emotion is useful

To cover up the probability that
The accuser fabricated the charge.

The accusation is
a magician's trick
turning attention
from the accuser's
bad intentions.

Those who would influence the thinking of
Millions of people understand that it's
Advantageous to begin with children
In the schools and to indoctrinate through

Graduation and those with the urge to
Control opinion have utilized the
Media and the screens of computers
And phones and tablets and televisions

And radio waves are broadcasting the
Bitterness of accusation either
Explicitly or implicitly and
Directly or anonymously and

Mixed with accidents and tragedies the
News is a dispiriting bombardment.

Controversy
accusation
hypnotize
lonely
fearful
people.

The radiation of sunlight that the
Earth is absorbing that is providing
The breath of life to each living being
And to each living being that has lived

And died anywhere in the cosmos that
We are aware of is only a small
Proportion of all the light that the sun
Produces as most of the energy

Radiates into space and mixes with
The trillions and trillions and trillions of
Other stars that are circling black holes
And I choose to believe the mystery

Of life and consciousness is beautiful
Even as life is so precarious.

There is no
explanation for
how the inorganic
became organic and how
beings became conscious.

Herbert London

Words of remembrance on the passing of
A friend are surprising gifts that we give
Each other and I knew Herbert as a
Writer in New York City and could not

Have known a lot about him and the list
Of his accomplishments was welcome but
It took a day for a story to emerge
From the bulk of information and to

Resonate that Herbert was scoring at
A pace surpassing his high school and league
Record when the basketball coach removed
Him and Herbert was outraged for many

Years until he absorbed the lesson of
Humility the coach had given him.

I learned
accomplishment
was founded upon
humility.

The river keeps flowing in the winter
Under three feet of ice on the surface
And water is moving consistently
And doesn't dawdle and doesn't hurry

And snow falling in the hollows and on
The limestone bluffs of the river valley
And on the streets and the homes of the town
Of Stillwater is snow for a season

But eventually the snow becomes
The river and then the river becomes
The ocean and then the ocean becomes
The clouds collecting and dispersing in

The sky until eventually the
Water drops and touches the earth again.

As I am drinking
water I am absorbing
the clouds the rain the
snow and the ice the river
and every ocean.

The sun is a balance of gravity
And nuclear fusion persisting for
Billions of years and it radiates in
Every direction and the proportion

Of its energy that warms the earth is
Minuscule — and compared with the trillions
And trillions of other stars it is an
Ordinary phenomenon from an

Analytical viewpoint — but given
The earth's orbit around the sun and the
Rotation of the earth on its axis
And the propitious distance of the

Earth from the sun the right formula of
Ingredients are here to foster life.

There are deserts and
tropical jungles and the
arctic poles and the
oceans and the prairies and
today today and today.

My life arises with my thoughts and I
Bestow proximity and context and
I choose which is magnificent and which
Is insignificant and with the choice

Of magnification I make desire
And repulsion and for me nothing does
Exist outside my awareness of it —
My consciousness is like a fire that lights

The distant cosmos — but when I have
My doubts I am a candle burning in
Darkness — and even with incandescence
There are shadows bordering my thinking —

I practice carefully to remember
There are consequences in my choices.

I am a sun
emanating
into mystery.

The Buddhists believe in the three poisons
Of greed anger and ignorance and we
Consider ignorance to be the source
Of much unnecessary suffering

And ignorance is more productive of
Harm than the most calculating anger
Because the ground of ignorance allows
For the arousal of anger and I

Appreciate that Buddhists don't condemn
Anyone and I am curious and
Am willing to practice every day to
Discover what I am ignorant of

And with my emotional waywardness
I will compose myself within patience.

There is
agitation
and
composure —
earth
and
heaven.

I suppose it happens given the fact
Of birth that there is a choice to be made
Given the never ending sequence of
Events and the fact that so much more than

Can be comprehended is happening
All at this moment here and extending
From here to infinity that the choice
Must be made whether I do believe that

An underlying order pervades the
Cosmos or that the cosmos is governed
By randomality and there is no
Point to compassion and benevolence

Beyond the gratification of me
And I might as well be a mosquito.

I decide without
giving the choice
much thought but
decide with huge
consequence.

I saw three crows in an oak tree on the
Way to my office when I glanced up and
Noticed a crow bobbing on a branch with
Its wings extended as it alighted

On the branch and I saw the other crows
Hopping and turning and then I drove on
Compelled by the chores I needed to do
But I wondered what the street and my car

Would look like from their perch in the oak —
And I questioned whether they have better
Eyes than I do — and could they be hungry —
And is one of them dominant — and the

Crows in a tree on an overcast day
Diverted me from useless obsession.

I was turning and
hopping in my head over
critical words
aimed at a fundraising
letter I had written.

I noticed a gathering of wax wings
In an apple tree and they were chirping
Excitedly together and being
A busybody I approached them and

Then they became quiet — I walked away
And they resumed chirping — and I returned
And they became quiet again while a
Few began protesting what could have been

Suspicion and irritation with my
Unwanted presence — and I remember
The many times I see various kinds
Of birds flying together and turning

Together in the same direction and —
Is it possible they are of one mind?

Perhaps together
they are the spirit
of a gossip
reincarnated
into wax wings.

A chickadee is in the bush outside
My window and others are flying to
The trees in the back yard and a layer
Of clouds is gradually moving and

The furnace is coming on to raise the
Temperature to a setting and then
It's quiet and perhaps my friend Jason
Is climbing the hundred cement steps in

Downtown Stillwater for the exercise
He enjoys and Steve could be attending
To the grandchildren he loves and there is
A girl somewhere I was entangled with

But it's a liberation for me not
To care where she is and what she's doing.

A black hole is
consuming a star
somewhere
but I am
quiet enough.

The tiny flakes of snow are descending
In a curving and meandering way
With enough accumulation over
The night for the thinnest layer of white

To be visible on the roofs of homes
And the barely noticeable snow that
Will not amount to much is giving the
Frigid air a texture under a gray

Sky and the diminished quality of the
Morning light is turning all the naked
Trees the same shade of a drab brown mixing
With the subdued greens of the pines and shrubs

And it's a pleasure for me to let these
Ordinary details envelope me.

The falling snow vanished —
the sky is gray but
the rim along the
far horizon is white.

That I was on the high school wrestling
Team forty-four years ago is a shock
To realize because I do not see
Myself as completely grown even though

I lived in Japan for nine years and was
Married for twenty-seven years and then
Divorced and both my kids are beyond the
Age of twenty-five-years-old and now I'm

Working in the home I grew up in and
Clearing the same driveway of snow that I
Cleared in high school and facing another
Winter and it seems like yesterday that

There were apple blossoms and lilacs and
The leaves were soaking in sunlight again.

Sometimes the
past seems like
yesterday and I
don't remember
what I've forgotten.

Wrestlers were expected to make weight
By late afternoon every Friday in
Preparation for a contest in the
Evening so the entirety of my

Week was aimed at stripping down naked and
Stepping on a scale and proving that I
Was one hundred and five pounds and on the
Preceding three days the morsels eaten

Only reminded me of how much I
Couldn't eat even with the leaning and
Lunging and lifting and leveraging
With all my might for six day of the week

And with my sweating in practice I was
Calculating how many pounds were off.

There were two hours
before the match reserved
for gorging and on
Saturday and Sunday
I discarded discipline.

I emerge from the earth as a fountain
Of thought and emotion and arising
With expression I flow in the creeks — and
Over rocks I am musical in the woods

And in an irresistible current
I roar between the boulders rapidly
And plunge into emptiness silently
And I gather with renewed strength onward

And in my broadness I carry the earth
In shades of brown and green and turquoise and
While moving with great force I am quiet
But my surface undulates ceaselessly —

I merge into oceans and atomize
Into clouds and drop again to the earth.

It's difficult
to surrender
identity and
direction and to
just flow.

Ice is forming on the river and the
Falling snow is turning the river white
And the open water in places looks
Dark and deadly — but I remember last

Summer the river was undulating
And sparkling under the summer sun
And I saw the swallows flitting along
The bank and over the river — and I

Remember a winter in Galveston
Watching the heavy grayness of the sky
And the white cresting waves of Galveston
Bay and I recall the seagulls wheeling

And wailing as I was pedaling my
Bike with the wind along the seawall.

Fluid
memory
arises in
glimpses.

I am a drop of consciousness playing
With words and my consciousness is like the
Blue of the sky today but the sky is
Much more than its blue appearance today

The sky also includes the rain and snow
And the thunder and lightning and
The wind that tears the leaves from the trees
In autumn — and the sky is also a

Part of the earthly circulation of
Rivers and oceans — and the sky transmits
The radiation of the sun — just as
I encompass loneliness and love and

Everything that did and could occur and
Everyone I did and could encounter.

I can't remember
everyone I've met
and can't account for
the traces of them that
live on in me.

I notice birds flying between the trees
Too far to see what types of birds they are —
I watch the sun rising and know it's the
Same sun that the Egyptians idolized —

I enjoy conversation with my friends
Because they tell me about their insights
And their maneuverings and I express
Myself and together we always laugh —

I believe we are spirits cycling
Through lifetimes on the earth and I return
To a mirror and see the face that I'm
Accustomed to and notice the wrinkles

About my eyes and I wonder with what
Other faces I have expressed my lives.

Does my original face
have features I am
accustomed to or does
it resemble
the sky?

I am practically minded and wear
The clothes the seasons demands — even though
I like to appear flamboyantly trim —
And in the winter I'm a blue jeans and

Polar fleece kind of guy who likes pockets
For carrying things as I am geared for
Getting things done — and as winter drags on
My boots become spattered with the salt that

The road crews use to melt the ice on the
Streets and it's a hassle to take off the
Boots and put on my shoes when entering
The house but I do it because it's not

Appropriate to tramp the snow and salt
Inside the house because I'm civilized.

In the winter
it's hard to keep
the weather from
intruding inside.

I know how to tap with my fingers and
Words appear on a screen in front of me
And if I get the first line correctly
The seed inside of the words will blossom —

I don't know when beginning what's inside
That needs getting out and in the middle
I don't know what the ending will be but
There is pleasure and satisfaction in

Balancing cadence grammar and meaning —
There is joy in selecting the words that
Carry impetus and intensity
Without wasting a single syllable

But at the end without a worthy point
The whole poem turns out to be a dud.

With effort and
consistency things
fit together and
I enjoy sharing
with people.

What is the red of the cardinal for?
What purpose does the scarlet serve beyond
The attraction of its mate? Does it live
Only for itself and its progeny?

Because I remember from my childhood
Taking such joy from the sight of the bird
As if its brilliant color transformed the
Drab gray skies the bare branches and the snow

On the ground into an enchanted land —
I would as well ask what is the winter
Solstice for that marks the passing of the
Longest nights and the turning to brighter

Days even though there are many dark days
Ahead when only the cardinal shines.

Childhood joy
and wonderment
from the sight of a
cardinal in winter is
unexplainable.

As a light snow is descending I am
Thinking about cherry blossoms and the
Tradition of writing about cherry
Blossoms in celebration of their blooms

And it is difficult to find something
Fresh to say about the blossoms because
So much has already been said over
The hundreds of years — but when the ground is

Frozen and the trees are sleeping and the
Wind is penetrating cherry petals
Are a vision of delicacy and
A reminder everything is moving

To a timely expression of essence
And beauty does appear persistently.

Cherry blossoms come
when the earth absorbs
the rain and the sun
returns to prominence.

More than in the middle of the summer
Trees express individuality
In the winter when the concealing leaves
Are absent and their forms are visible

And I can see every crook and curve — and
There are the evergreen trees and the shrubs
And as I'm driving about I can see
The differences between the maples

Elms and the oaks but each tree has its own
Way of reaching the sun — and I've noticed
Their common drab brown but today I see
That this one has dignity and that one

Is disheveled and this cottonwood is
Thin while another was struck by lightning.

The trees are a
quiet presence but
with winter wind
they resonate with
motion.

The story of Christ didn't begin in
Bethlehem where a baby was born in
A stable to parents of humble means
In a country strewn with rocks and sand and

Where the Roman Empire was the latest
Victor in a succession of trials of
A people — there was the prophesy and
Yearning for a savior in the midst of

Hardship and emptiness — and the people
Wanted a Messiah and they waited
Patiently while burdened with sorrows and
They needed a gentle master who would

Reveal the meaning of their suffering
And who could summon the strength within them.

The joy of the
Annunciation
and the birth
of the Christ
is fresh today.

It's a fear of mine and maybe yours too —
To be thrown away by people I love
When they know me better than anyone
Does and they are familiar with who I

Am — and there are memories of all the
Fun and I recall the Christmas morning
When I was given to Pamela and
She squealed with joy and had to be with me

For all of a glorious winter — but
The years have passed and Pamela gives her
Attention to her phone and no one looks
At me except to shuck me here and there

And it was not my fault that the cat has
Peed on me — and they really could wash me.

Here I am
Mr. Teddy Bear
on the trash container
by the street
being dumped.

The snow in the night was expected in
My neighborhood but the temperature
Rose through the early hours and by dawn
The snow was slush and difficult to move

But the several inches had to be moved
Because eventually watery
Snow will freeze and adhere to the driveway
As a gnarly hazard — the snow blower

Clogged so I kept my legs moving and scraped
With the shovel as if I were a plow
Clearing the street and when I was finished
Water was flowing on the street — and it

Rained all day and into the next night and
Just before dawn a cold front had arrived.

I can muster my
best efforts but
sometimes a
coating of ice is
unavoidable.

On the occasion of New Year's Day in
Minnesota the trees are dormant and
Their roots are embedded in the frozen
Earth and their branches extending to their

Twigs are motionless under a gray sky
And for them the winter days and months are
Meaningless but for me they are symbols
Of a rhythm of a lifetime in a

Season of bareness — and what a weight the
Stories I remember about my past
Are — and my memories are like roots and
They would be able to hold me firmly

In place if I weren't aware the past is
Gone and I can grow into the future.

The nurturing sun
radiates a life giving
rhythm of seasons
and I choose to believe in
open possibilities.

There are so many choices to make in
The hours of a day and although I
Am often awake — and go to sleep
At the same time — and I rely on a

Predictable schedule — and I know
With good probability where I will
Be and what I will be doing at a
Certain time of day — there is always the

Possibility I could stop and drop
What I am doing — and perhaps that's what's
Meant by being spontaneous — that I
Could do something that I've never done before —

There are so many choices in a day
And dissatisfaction can be helpful.

It takes a little
pain to be poised
and be creative enough
to exploit a
possibility.

Google and Facebook

Somehow Google engineers have harnessed
All the data on the Internet — and
So many people use the Internet
For business and for pleasure and because

Google controls the access to so much
Information Google is powerful —
If I want to know who Svengali was
Or where the nearest Chinese restaurant is

I can type a question and Google will
Inform me — and when I want directions
For driving somewhere Google Maps directs
Me with satellites orbiting the earth —

Google appears to be an all-knowing
Helper who is always available.

The phone I carry
in a pocket with
Google apps is like
a genie who gratifies
unlimited desires.

It doesn't matter what the intentions
Of the Google executives are or
Whether their denials are genuine
Or that they are merely a business and

Lack the power of a government — it
Is true many Google apps embedded
Within the phones that people carry are
Recording where people are going and

What they are doing — and it is true in
Order to gain access to a vast and
Lucrative market the Google big shots
Are willing to magnify the power

Of the Chinese government to observe
Every keystroke the Chinese people make.

The technology
of enveloping
inescapable
surveillance is
being refined.

There was a news report yesterday that
Revealed Facebook has been sharing the
Private messages of its users with
Google and other panjandrums of the

Internet making me nervous that my
Expressions of myself are rippling
Into algorithms manifesting
Into categories established by

Businesses who want to sell me stuff — and
Becoming a data point for profit
Doesn't bother me that much as long as
The offerings are something I might like

But the interpenetration of our
Humanity is becoming scary.

Electronics
and my keystrokes
are revealing my
personality to
to strangers.

There is visibility but also
Remoteness on Facebook that appears to
Make people anywhere touchable and
I am in the habit of exploring

The world and I love the videos of
Elephants and lions and eagles and
I enjoy the acrobatics people
Do and it's easy to forget that I'm

Separated from people and absorbed
In a pixilated screen and as I
Am selecting which postings that I like
The system is providing more of what

I like almost as if I were in an
Animated friendly conversation.

Is Facebook an
electronic
pixilated
opium den?

I play with words and the inspiration
That comes brings energy that carries me
Through the day — and I post my poems on
Facebook sharing my enthusiasm

And I aim for discernment and humor
Filtering my perceptions into as
Few words as possible so that each word
Carries more impact than it normally

Does — and I am mixing the better part
Of my consciousness into the vast and
Intimidating darkness of cyber
Space and my postings are like pebbles that

I'm tossing into a ceaseless ocean
Of swelling and rolling and thundering.

I do my best and
don't worry about
consequences — being
a particle and
a wave.

It's a worthy practice to open my
Perceptions to whatever comes my way
But I select my daily momentum
And with every step I am burdened

With the habits and stories I use to
Explain my experience to myself —
And it is a worthy ambition to
Leave behind as much of me as I can —

And I aspire to comprehend the
Impact of the endless and the boundless
Manifestation of this instant now —
Because before now things were different

And after now things will never be the
Same — and I don't want to use a filter.

I lose myself
with videos
of places I
will never be
on Facebook.

The tallest waterfall on the earth was
Found by a frustrated Jimmy Angel
After his puny plane got stuck in the
Mud on Tabletop Mountain and maybe

He was awestruck by the water plunging
The three thousand feet into a canyon
To be named Devil's Canyon but he walked
For eleven days in the jungle of

Venezuela before he was rescued
And he didn't find the gold he wanted
But the falls were named the Angel Falls for
Him — and I learned of the Angel Falls by

Watching a video on Facebook which
Is not being there but almost as good.

When the water
is plunging into
empty space
is it silent or
does it sound?

Lacking
wisdom and
discretion where
will Google and
Facebook lead us?

Aslan

I love the morning because Aslan the
Mighty created the morning with a
Deep and triumphant voice and as he was
Singing the sound reverberated from

Every direction and with the singing
The stars the moon and the earth appeared and
There was a fresh wind and a light on the
Horizon and hills became visible and

The sky was becoming white and pink and
Gold and Aslan's voice was rising shaking
The air swelling to crescendo and
Summoning compelling impetus and

The first sun rose revealing a valley
With a broad river flowing to the east.

Aslan the lion
shaggy and immense
was facing the sun.

There were mountains in the south and smaller
Hills in the north and the land was raw and
Empty and as Aslan was pacing and
Lilting his song was rippling away

Over the earth and as he was pacing
The valley was greening with grass and the
Grass was moving up the hills like a wave
And the grass was cresting on the mountain

Slopes and the valley was becoming dark
With heather — and bristles with spiky limbs
Were reaching to the sky and sprouting dots
Of leaves — and with a prolonged series of

Notes there were willows along the river
And willow leaves were flowing in the wind.

The branches of a
fully grown beech were
swaying in a breeze
and rhododendron and
wild roses were blooming.

In creation Narnia was bursting
With growth and Narnia was peopled with
Fauns and satyrs and naiads and centaurs
And talking trees and animals and the

Beavers were industrious and the dogs
Were exuberant and all the beings
With the gift of speech were also gifted
With innocence but coincident with

The birthing of life was the intrusion
Of a witch who introduced evil to
The land after she was released from a
Spell when a human boy named Digory

In another world on the verge of doom
Was taken with a moment's temptation.

Curiosity
led Digory to
ring a bell inside
a ruined castle
and release Jadis.

Aslan was aware of Jadis because
Aslan is maker and master — and he
Knew that Jadis was responsible for
The deaths of everyone in the kingdom

Of Charn and that Jadis would dominate
Narnia in the future — and Aslan
Knew what Digory had done and saw that
Digory was lured into a journey

Between worlds by an uncle who was too
Cowardly to go while Digory's Mom
Was dying in bed and his Dad was in
India — and compassion and justice

Were evident even as Aslan was
Lighting the stars and raising the first sun.

Aslan touched noses
with the beasts and the touching
created talking
elephants and antelope
beavers giraffes and horses.

Jadis escaped while Aslan was busy
With Narnia and after Aslan gave the
The gift of speech to a selection of
Animals Digory found his courage

And asked Aslan to heal his mother and
Digory was surprised that Aslan was
Crying with tears of grief for Digory's
Mother but Aslan said since Digory

Had played a part in bringing evil to
Narnia Digory must do a task to
To mitigate the harm — it's curious
That Aslan the mighty would ask a boy

To answer for his human frailty
When Aslan could have done the task himself.

Digory was to
ride a flying horse over
the western mountains
to a garden and pick an
apple from the tree of life.

A wall surrounded the garden and an
Inscription was on the gate warning that
The garden may be entered only by
The gate and the fruit be taken only

For others or forborne and otherwise
A thief would grasp his heart's desire and
Despair and Digory felt the truth of
The words and entered by the gate and he

Took a silver apple as Aslan asked —
To be given to Aslan — and he looked
At the apple and smelled it and a thirst
Came over him and he thought who would know

If he ate one and took another and
With effort he put it in his pocket.

Jadis was inside
the wall and her mouth
was stained with juice and
she was arrogant
even triumphant.

It was the apple of youth from the tree
Of life and Jadis asked why retrieve it
For the lion for the lion to eat
When Digory could taste it and be young

Forever and together they could be
King and Queen of Narnia — or he could
Return to London to his mother and
Could slice the apple into pieces and

Could see his mother's color return as
She ate and she would sleep with healing and
Wake refreshed — and what had the lion done
For him that he should be the lion's slave —

And what would his mother think if she knew
That he could have saved her but he wouldn't?

"Look what the lion
has done — he has made
you as heartless and
as cruel as he is."

"And what business do you have in this world
And what could that beast of a lion do
To you when you return to your own world?"
Asked Jadis but Digory remembered

His mother and knew that she would want him
To honor his promise and there was a
Meanness palpable in the witch's words
That determined his choice and Digory

Abandoned the witch but carried doubt and
Sorrow with him flying east on the horse
Over the mountains and wooded hills and
Past the cliffs and waterfall and evening

Shadow was falling on the plains as he
Took courage remembering Aslan's tears.

The flying horse landed
And nymphs and fauns
parted as Digory
approached and gave
the apple to Aslan.

With a pervasive voice Aslan exclaimed
"Well done!" and everyone in Narnia
Heard him — and Aslan asked Digory to
Throw the apple and seed the soil with its

Magic — and a tree grew as swiftly as
A flag rises and its branches cast a
Light and a wholesome fragrance arose and
Silver apples appeared like the stars and

Aslan asked the Narnians to guard the
Tree as a shield against Jadis because
She would become quite formidable but
The tree would repel her for hundreds of

Years — Jadis seized an apple for herself
And was careless of the consequences.

With no ending of
strength and life
misery will persist
forever.

"Because the magic works according to
Its nature a stolen apple would have
Healed your mother and would have given her
An endless and unhappy life that both

Of you would have regretted but now take
An apple from the tree — and though it will
Not bestow eternal life in your world
It will heal her — and destroy the magic

Rings your uncle used — you do not need them
When I am with you" said Aslan and he
Shook his mane and Digory was floating
In a sea of tossing gold — and sweetness

And power rolled about him and he felt
So happy wise and good — and quite awake.

Digory peeled the
apple of youth and
his mother ate it
piece by piece and
then she slept.

Clive Staples Lewis was an officer
In the British army who survived the
Brutality of World War One as a
Bitter atheist but while he was a

Don teaching literature at Oxford
University he converted to
Christianity and he developed
A facility for writing stories

For children to pass on the faith that was
Inspiring him and he created
Aslan the benevolent and the wise
Lion and Aslan with masterful love

Composed the elements into order
And the kingdom of Narnia appeared.

Every morning is
pristine with the first light of
the sun spreading
over the country even
on a cloudy winter day.

Appearances

I desire to present myself as a
Vision of trimness and in the light of
The afternoon I see how well I did
Shaving in the morning by looking in

The mirror attached to back side of
The sun visor flap while I am sitting
Behind the steering wheel of my car and
I often find the persistency of

The hair on my chin and under my nose
Disturbingly visible but what is
Quite distressing is the obstinacy
Of the hair along the insides of my

Nostrils and just under my nose where it's
Difficult to maneuver the razor.

Every day
I angle in the
corner of my clipper
with its sharp little teeth
buzzing excitedly.

The preliminaries take place as soon
As I leave the shower as a steaming
Pink something and I make sure the right leg
Goes in the right hole of my shorts and that

The shorts are forward to back so that my
Appurtenance is snug and then I note
The label of the t-shirt because it
Needs to be front to back and the pulling

On and taking off and then pulling on
Again is frustrating if I'm wrong the
First time and the label shows me the back
Side and then comes the pulling buckling

And zipping of my jeans and I apply
Deodorant and cologne to be me.

Going through the day
with my t-shirt on
backwards would be like
pushing against the
wind every minute.

I like to squeeze as much as possible
Of the toothpaste out of the tube because
I'm the kind of guy who pretends that he
Doesn't waste anything — although I do

Spend money impulsively so maybe
My toothpaste etiquette serves as a salve
For a guilty conscience — and when most of
The paste has been extruded I like to

Pinch the end of tube with my fingers
Across the seam and I squeeze the tube to
Absolute flatness and roll it up for
Day after day squeezing and rolling with

Joy until I reach the rigid round top
Where it's hard to get the last of the paste.

It is a
reliable
revelation
how long
I delay the
inevitable.

The most dignified personage has to
Pull on his socks and perhaps it is true
He is not aware of the dosage of
Humble pie he is digesting but in

The act he is just an ordinary
Guy — and I had forgotten the pranks I
Pulled in high school until a happenstance
Discussion with a friend reminded me

I used to wear different color socks
And when brave I wore blue and white to gauge
The depth of attention in passing and
Sometimes I would be subtle with green and

Brown and on other days almost normal
With the lightest and darkest shades of blue.

Popularity
escaped me and
I thought nobody
noticed but obviously
I was wrong.

Perhaps the makers of round shoelaces
Are as ignorant and incurious
As their product suggests that they may be
Or perhaps they are just laughing at us

Because the round laces of every pair
Of boots I have ever owned come undone
At least a half dozen times a day — and
I have the indignity of bending

Over in public and tying a lace
Again knowing it will stay tied only
Temporarily — and I must weigh the
Frustration and the embarrassment with

The inconvenience of departing from
My routine and tramping to a shoe store.

There is the
satisfaction of
ripping the laces out
and tossing them
in a trash can.

Minnesota winters are cruel to the
Appendages as the moisture in the
Air vanishes and I awake to the
Painful cracking of my finger tips and

Of my lips and once cracked there's the lengthy
Healing to endure so I prepare while
Getting dressed with lotion on my hands and
Balm on my lips and when leaving home I'm

Wrapped like an eggroll in a polar fleece
And in a jacket with a hood for the
Coldest days that protects my ears and with
Mittens for my fingers — and my toes are

Swaddled within knitted socks and arctic
Boots — and only my nose remains exposed.

My nose is the
foremost part of me
and it has to be
very cold to breathe
with frozen nostrils.

Not every winter day requires the
Complete rigmarole of protection
And on the milder days I engage a
Sense of peacock flamboyance and I may

Choose among an array hats and leave
My ears hanging out and I could select
A brimmed wool fedora imitating
Fred Astaire or I could don my salmon

Proud militant hat from Afghanistan
Looking like two pancakes but normally
I choose between my French berets because
They project a careless jaunty image

And I may pull the floppy hat leftward
Or rightward or backwards as it suits me.

Often I do meld
with the bare trees with my
tan brown black berets
but sometimes I flaunt myself
with blue and green and burgundy.

When snow is
descending constantly
in tiny flakes and
accumulating quickly
everything is covered.

— *Tekkan*

www.ingramcontent.com/pod-product-compliance
Lightning Source LLC
Chambersburg PA
CBHW052102070526
44584CB00017B/2292